THE ALPS

PHOTOGRAPHS BY

Yoshikazu Shirakawa

TEXT BY

Max A. Wyss

INTRODUCTION BY

Chris Bonington

THE ALPS

Harry N. Abrams, Inc., Publishers, New York

Translated from the German *Majestät der Alpen* by J. Maxwell Brownjohn

Library of Congress Cataloging in Publication Data

Shirakawa, Yoshikazu, 1935–
    The Alps: photographs.

    First published in Japan under title: Arupusu.
    1. Alps—Description and travel—Views. I. Wyss,
Max Albert. II. Title.
DQ823.S4713   1975   914.94′7′047   74-30304
ISBN 0-8109-0272-9

Library of Congress Catalogue Card Number: 74-30304
Published by Harry N. Abrams, Incorporated, New York, 1975
Printed and bound in Switzerland by C. J. Bucher AG, Lucerne

Introduction

The Alps stretch in a tight-drawn bow for five hundred miles, from the Mediterranean to the Adriatic; a mountain spine which has helped to determine the history of Europe throughout the ages and which today provides the most developed mountain playground in the world. It was also the birth-place of both mountaineering and skiing as sports.

Within its comparatively small area is an incredible range of mountain scenery, rock and glacial forms and types; the brown granite of the Mont Blanc massif, with its aiguilles, steep snow and rock faces; the limestone of the Oberland, with its brooding North Walls; the great snow peaks of the Valais and, across to the East, the sheer or overhanging limestone walls of the Dolomites. No other mountain range in the world is so accessible and at the same time has such a variety of mountain experience to offer.

There are records back into the Middle Ages of men going into the mountains, but in most instances these were crystal-seekers, hunters, traders or pilgrims, searching for a pass which would give them a short-cut from one valley to the next. Few felt the urge to reach a summit, though as early as 1492 Mont Aiguille, near Grenoble, was ascended on the orders of Charles VIII of France. It was not until the end of the eighteenth century that any further interest was shown in reaching the summit of any mountain; it was then that local men from Chamonix began to tackle some of the peaks in the environs of Mont Blanc and finally, after several attempts, Mont Blanc was climbed by Michel Gabriel Paccard and Jacques Balmat in 1786. Other ascents followed, but these tended to be isolated events, the aim being to stand at the highest point of Europe, with the way of reaching this point being almost immaterial. Climbing as a sport, with a group of participants coming back to the mountains over a period of time, to pioneer or repeat climbs, only started in the mid-nineteenth century. The early mountaineers were almost all wealthy people who could afford the leisure and the money to travel to the Alps. They were undoubtedly helped by the new rail system which enabled them to make the journey across Europe comparatively quickly. They were, perhaps, escaping from the grime and machines of the industrial cities of Europe.

It was these newcomers, rather than the mountain-dwellers, who provided the initiative, but the local men had an important influence on the early development of climbing in the Alps. They already knew the way on to the glaciers and the lower slopes of the mountains, and were therefore employed as guides. Until the end of the nineteenth century they were to dominate the sport, providing the tactical leadership and judgment for most of the pioneering parties.

By 1865 most of the four-thousand-metre peaks of the Alps had been climbed and several had been ascended by more than one route. Equipment was still primitive by modern standards: the rope was a length of hemp, and the use of it to safeguard the party adequately was barely understood. The alpenstock was big and cumbersome and the climbs that were attempted were little more than scrambling by modern-day standards.

In 1865 the outstanding challenge was the Matterhorn. The race to climb it was as competitive, and dramatic, as any present-day climbing saga. Edward Whymper and Charles Hudson tackled it from the North by the Hornli Ridge, Louis Carrel from the South, both on the same day. Whymper won the race for the summit but then, on the way down, tragedy struck: four of the party of seven slipped to their deaths.

The new sport was treated to harsh words in the Press, *The Times* writing: 'Why is the best blood of England to waste itself in scaling hitherto inaccessible peaks, in staining the eternal snow and reaching the unfathomable abyss never to return?'

But climbers were not deterred, and in the remaining years of the nineteenth century tackled increasingly difficult routes on peaks, most of which had already been climbed. British mountaineers took a leading role in this development and the Alpine Club, which was formed in 1857, was the doyen of European climbing clubs. Unfortunately it also proved to be a stultifying influence on British climbing in the first half of the twentieth century, for it demanded from the start both climbing and social qualifications. The Alpine Clubs of the other European countries, on the other hand, were only concerned with their members' interest in mountaineering.

It was partly as a result of this hidebound attitude that British mountaineers seemed less able to adapt themselves to change and development in mountaineering ethics and techniques in the early twentieth century. At the end of the nineteenth century climbers in the Eastern Alps were beginning to tackle the sheer limestone walls of the Austrian Alps and the Dolomites. Men like the Italian, Angelo Dibona, were beginning to use pitons and a more effective rope technique to overcome these challenges. At the end of the First World War an increasing number of young climbers from the cities immediately bordering the Alps began to use these techniques to tackle the steep walls of the Western Alps.

Climbers had already begun to abandon the use of guides, on account of the cost, as much as on the grounds of simple adventure. The British pioneers, A.F. Mummery and Geoffrey Wynthrop Young, tackled new and difficult routes without guides, and the post-war climbers started using bold, controversial new techniques. The North Wall of the Eiger was attempted; eight men died before the route was finally climbed, and inevitably, the attempts were heavily and sensationally covered in the press; the first ascent for example, was castigated as a symbol of Nazism. The methods used on this, and similar hard climbs in the Western Alps, were condemned in the Alpine Club *Journal* by its formidable editor, Colonel Strutt. Commenting on the first ascent of the Capucin de la Brenva he wrote:'this sort of exploit is quite beyond the pale, and is a degradation of mountaineering. Any steeple-jack could have done the work better, and in a tenth of the time.'

Between the wars British climbers took only a limited part in the development of technical climbing, though they were extremely active in the greater mountain-ranges of the world. It was only after the Second World War that a new generation of climbers, drawn from every kind of background, broke away from the traditional attitudes of the Alpine Club which condemned the use of pitons and modern techniques, and started to repeat the climbs already achieved by leading Continental climbers. The vanguard of this new development were young climbers from the universities, Hamish Nichol and Tom Bourdilion particularly; they made the first British ascents of such routes as the West Face of the Aiguille Noire de Peuterie and the East Face of the Capucin in the early nineteen-fifties. They were quickly followed by two Mancunian plumbers, Joe Brown and Don Whillans, who made the fourth ascent of the West Face of the Drus and then a new route, the West Face of the Blaitière, which even today has the reputation of being one of the hardest rock climbs in the Mont Blanc area.

Since the mid-fifties, British climbers have tackled almost all the hardest routes in the Alps and have contributed a certain number of first ascents. Since the early days of the sport the experts have bemoaned at the end of each phase, that the Alps have been 'climbed out', that everything worth doing has been done, only to be proved wrong by each succeeding generation. But today this state of affairs has almost been reached. Every ridge and Face has a route on it, sometimes more than one, and most of these routes have already been climbed solo. There are queues on all the popular climbs; bolt ladders have been hammered up the blank walls of the Dolomites; the mountains are full of refuges resembling hotels more than simple huts; helicopters hover among the peaks, ready to come to the rescue of any climber who has got into difficulty, while cable-cars reach into the heart of the mountains. As a result, more and more climbers are venturing into the Alps in the winter, seeking a solitude impossible to attain in the summer; to tackle routes already made as summer ascents, or new lines too dangerous in summer because of stonefall.

Today the pioneer must go off to far-away mountain-ranges. Yet the magic of the Alps can still be found. If you can escape the crowds by discovering a little-known rock or ice wall, or ski into a secluded valley, then they suddenly assume a stature as magnificent as that of any mountain range in the world.

CHRIS BONINGTON

Glacier-light

How raced the heart within my breast
despite my youthful wanderlust
when, turning homeward, I did view
the snow-clad peaks soft swathed in blue,
   the great and silent radiance!

With avid breath I drank in fast
the market's fumes, the city's dust.
I saw life's battle. What say you,
my purest glacier-light, thereto,
   you great and silent radiance?

This question, posed over a hundred years ago by Conrad Ferdinand Meyer, is more troubling than ever before. The modern world, characterized by the poet as 'the market's fumes, the city's dust', is choking humanity and making it hard to breathe, physically and mentally. People everywhere are pining for a return to Nature, but not in a spirit of Rousseauesque sentimentality or romantic emotionalism. What is at stake is the preservation of man himself and his survival in the civilized world.

Up in the glacier-light of the Alps lies the precise antithesis of civilization: the elemental

25

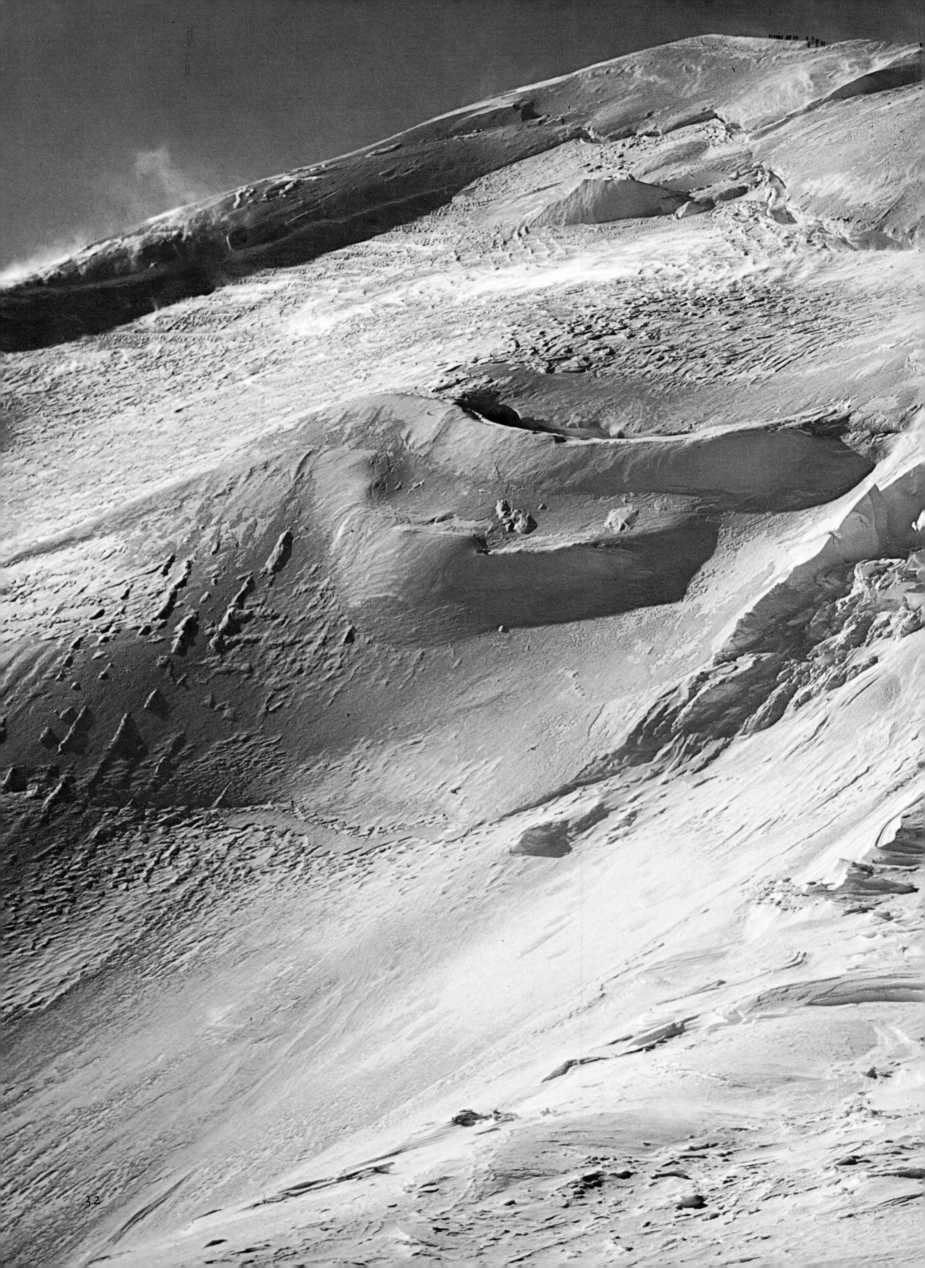

and primeval world which has so far evaded subjugation by man and remains a realm where he is still confronted by the raw strength of Nature and compelled to rely on himself, on his own intellectual, spiritual and physical resources. The huge alpine range, which rises from the sea that laps the Côte d'Azur and extends to where the Leopoldsberg drops to the Danube north of Vienna, forms the backbone of Europe. The Alps divide Western Europe into north and south, both culturally and geographically, and have played their part in European history since Hannibal's day. Mountains have always influenced people, neighbouring races as well as native highlanders, not only in the geographic and topographic sense but politically and economically too. Half-barrier, half-link, they have governed or helped to determine political events and national destinies. Military gambles by Hannibal, Napoleon or Suvorov were won or lost in alpine passes. The toll paid by Hannibal's cavalry, Napoleon's troops and the Russian army was a tribute to the brute force of the mountains. Only those who have felt the razor-edged wind sweep through an alpine pass on a winter's day can gauge the sufferings and despair of a soldier in the Napoleonic army.

Thanks to the awesome reputation of the Alps Lowlanders were long deterred from visiting or exploring their rocky, ice-bound wastes. At a time when British and Dutch merchant-men were ploughing the oceans and opening up new continents, wide expanses of alpine terrain were still blank patches on the maps of Europe. Although men had always inhabited the mountains, first as hunters and later as farmers and cattle-breeders, they clung to the valleys and sparse alpine pastures in dread of the sinister natural forces, alias evil spirits and dragons, that dwelt amid the crags and ice-girt ravines. The boldest of these valley-dwellers soon found their way across natural passes, established bridle-paths, scaled walls of rock and defied raging torrents in quest of a route to the south, where wheat flourished, grapes ripened and life seemed easier and gayer. Two thousand years ago, Rome was linked with its provinces in Western Gaul and the Celtic North by way of alpine passes which served as strategic military roads, supply and trade routes. They led past towering walls of rock and menacing glaciers at whose foot mountain-dwellers eked out a wretched existence. There must even then have been daring hunters who ventured on to glaciers, pursued their quarry into vast ravines and were tempted to defy the ice and conquer the highest rocky pinnacle. Many of them failed to return, having been crushed by falling stones, swept away by avalanches or paralysed by the cold. The object of temptation remained, however, almost within reach yet infinitely remote. As one mountain guide is reported to have said: *I cha nid angersch!* (I can't help myself).

True credit for the exploration of the Alps must go to scientists and scholars. They were attracted not so much by a desire for the experience of natural phenomena as by the idea of geographic and topographic research. Johann Jakob Scheuchzer wrote his *Naturgeschichte der schweizerischen Gebirge* in 1716; *Voyages dans les Alpes*, by the eminent Genevese scholar and mountaineer Horace Bénédict de Saussure, appeared between 1779 and 1796, and trigono-metrical measurements to determine the height of well-known peaks in the canton of Berne were made in 1790 by Johann Georg Tralles, professor of mathematics and teacher of natural philosophy at Berne Academy. As early as 1777 a comprehensive guide to the Bernese Ober-land was published. Its author, the clergyman Jakob Samuel Wyttenbach, compiled it 'for use by the numerous travellers... who desire to visit the alps and glaciers and whom he seeks to inform how such journeys are to be arranged and how benefit may be derived therefrom'. The existence of such a guide proves that alpine tours were socially in vogue at this period; the romance of travel had found an alluring objective in the Alps, and 'trips to the mountains' had begun. Alpine tours formed part of the educational programme of an enlightened, though romantically inclined social class. Goethe and Karl August Duke of Weimar used Wyttenbach's guide on their Swiss travels, and if Goethe was inspired to write 'Gesang der Geister über den Wassern' after seeing the Staubbach waterfall, some of the credit should go to the Bernese clergyman. It may be added, that Felix Mendelssohn-Bartholdy somewhat spitefully remarked in a letter written fifty or so years later: 'I find it incomprehensible, like many other things in this world, that Goethe could write nothing from Switzerland save a few weak poems and some even weaker letters...' Prominent and highly placed visitors to the Bernese Oberland, a much favoured place at that time, used to be fittingly received and entertained on an official basis. When Friedrich Albert, Margrave of Brandenburg, visited 'the glacier' during a lengthy visit to Switzerland in 1690 and lodged at Interlaken, where he dined four times, the district exchequer recorded the cost of the nobleman's stay as '166 livres and 13 batzen'. In the autumn of the same year the glaciers of Grindelwald were visited by the English envoy Mr Coxe, his wife and retinue. Expenses, which were borne by the Bernese government, amounted to 120 crowns. At Grindelwald alone, Mr Coxe's party and their 35 horses accounted for 150 sovereigns' worth of food, wine, oats and barley. It may be added that the English not only formed the majority of visitors to the Alps during the next two centuries, but introduced something which might be described as modern mountaineering. The ice-clad alpine peaks remained inviolate for a long time to come, however. Souvenirs of the Swiss Alps were much in demand and those who had not been all the way to the top took care to acquire at least a likeness of the romantic alpine world as supplied by the local painters. In good years, an artist such as J.L. Aberli (1723-86) was reputed to sell coloured drawings to the value of 2,000 louis d'or in Berne alone. Humbler visitors contented themselves with pressed mountain flowers or pieces of rock-crystal of the sort which could now be purchased almost everywhere, down in the valleys as well as up in the mountains. Wilhelm Gerhard speaks in his *Spaziergang über die Alpen* (1824) of a curio shop housed in a small hut on the summit of the Montanvert, above Chamonix: 'Wine and cold roast chamois we had brought with us. The attendant there manages the mountain dairy and, at the same time, tempts visitors' purses with a stand displaying small collections of minerals and plants, seals, necklaces, ear-rings and snuff-boxes of cut crystal. The rock-crystal is found in large quantities in a neighbouring cave on the Col du Géant. Stuffed chamois and ibexes, together with bas-reliefs of varied size representing the Mont Blanc range and the entire Chamonix valley can be cheaply acquired at small shops.'

A century and a half after Gerhard's mountain tour, the modern visitor may think what he will of the souvenir shops that abound in mountain resorts. There will come a time when, emotionally stirred by the alpine sunrise or afterglow, he is glad to find at least a postcard on which to scrawl a memento, however inadequate, of his time in the mountains. Funds seldom run to anything more, for carved chamois and ibexes are expensive, and edelweiss protected. Rock-crystal is heavy, yet it is just what many tourists long to acquire, perhaps because it embodies the essence of the mountains.

The White Giant

Mountains have often been endowed with something akin to a personality, and sometimes even a name to go with it. The German-speaking inhabitants of a mountainous area generally confined themselves to calling their local peak the *Horn*. Every enthusiast knows, for example, that there is a Matterhorn, a Weisshorn and a Rheinwaldhorn. *Hörner* are as numerous as the *dents* of the Western Alps, those fangs of rock which bear names such as *du Diable*, *du Géant* or *du Caïman*. No one really knows how the triple constellation of the Eiger, Mönch and Jungfrau acquired its names, or why the Watzmann or La Marmolata should be called what they are and not something else. But there is one mountain, a white giant 4,807 metres tall, which became known simply as Mont Blanc.

To the people of Chamonix, it was simply there, vast, inaccessible, unconquered and wrapped in a remoteness which could not be expressed in words. But it was there to be conquered. When the two Chamoniards Jacques Balmat and Dr Paccard climbed it for the first time in 1786, the result was a European sensation and people remained unconvinced that the pair had really performed so incredible a feat until de Saussure confirmed it in 1787. Hundreds, indeed thousands, followed their example in the years to come. Anyone who regarded himself as a mountain-lover and mountaineer had to scale the peak of peaks. Chamonix, with its growing number of guides, became the headquarters of Europe's first mountaineering centre. The Guild of Guides not only won fame and prestige but amassed a considerable fortune.

Among the early mountaineers was an aristocratic lady named Henriette d'Angeville. According to a contemporary account she had grown up in the country, loved Nature and used to undertake numerous tours in the Jura. It was in July 1838 that Mademoiselle d'Angeville visited Chamonix, bent on finally carrying out her long-cherished plan to climb Mont Blanc. She returned to Geneva to prepare for the expedition. When, after several days of bad weather, she glimpsed the white summit of the 'monarch' from the Ile Rousseau, 'her heart pounded furiously, deep sighs escaped her breast, and she felt a burning desire to ascend (it) which thrilled her to the tips of her toes'. By then a spinster of forty-four, Henriette d'Angeville remained adamant even when an English friend, Lady Cullum, tearfully pleaded with her to abandon the ill-omened venture. She made her will, solicited her physician's advice on how to comport herself both during and after the climb, and set off for Chamonix, where she alighted at the Hôtel de l'Union. Couttet, the chief guide, was instructed to engage five guides in addi-

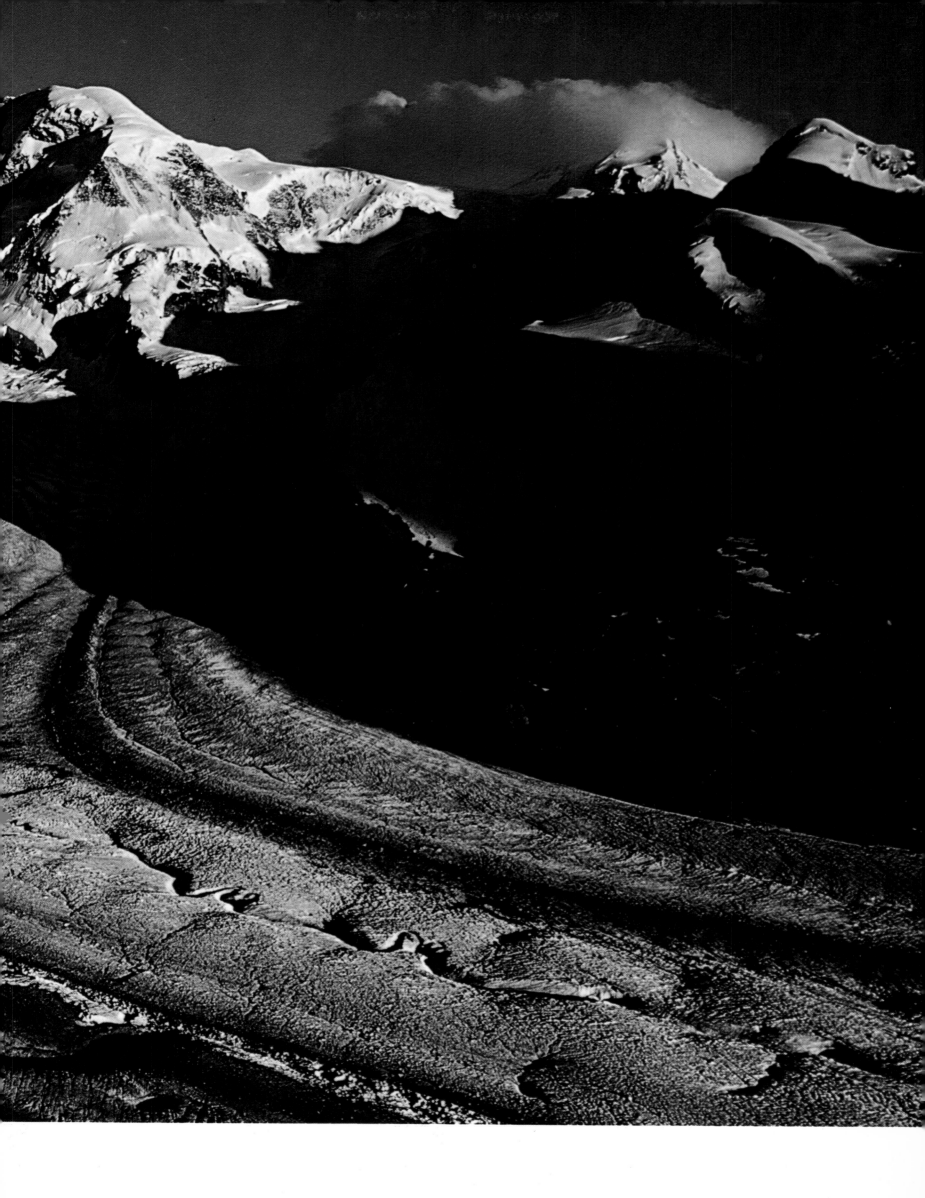

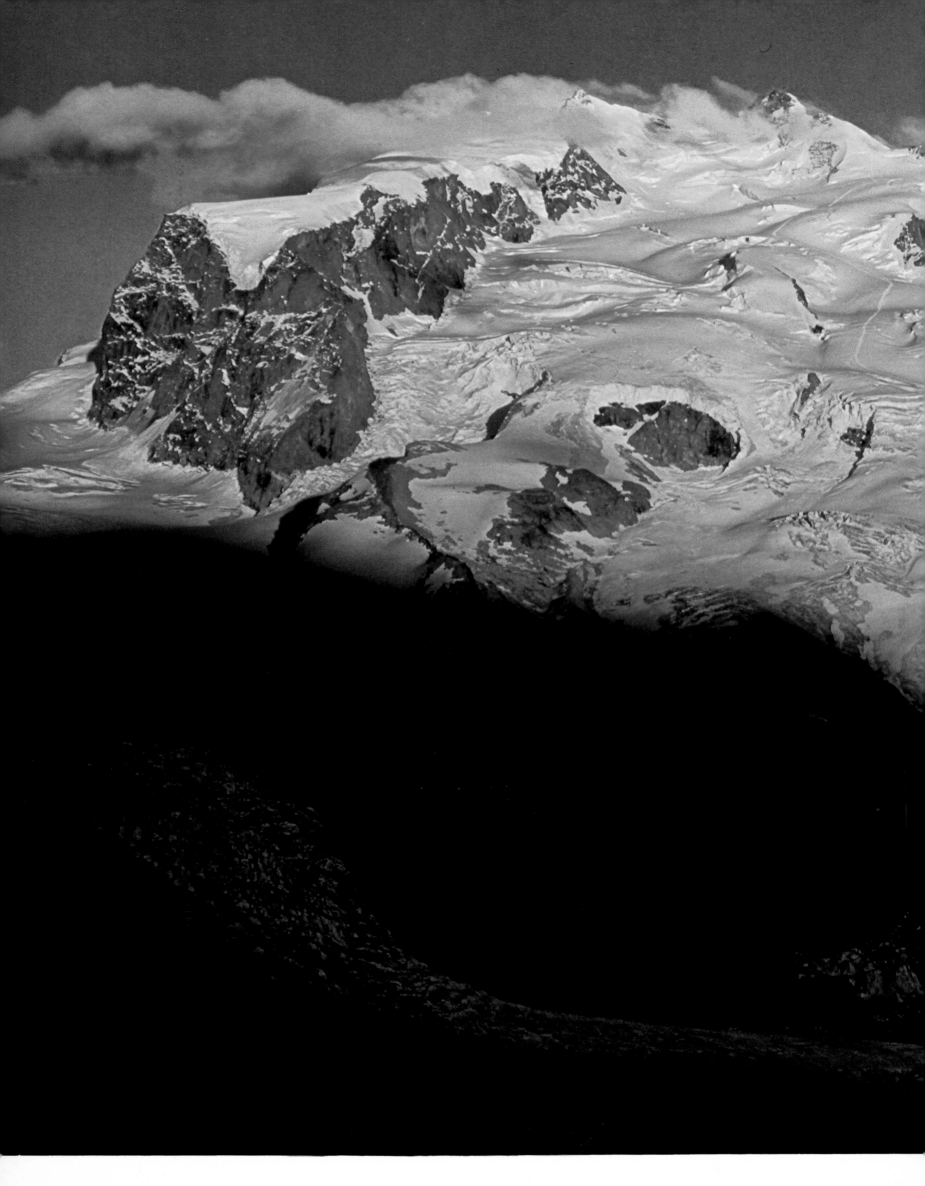

72

tion to himself, and half-a-dozen porters. The expedition's list of supplies is worth a glance. It included 2 legs of mutton, 2 ox-tongues, 24 fowl, 6 loaves of bread weighing 3-4 pounds each, 18 bottles of claret, 1 bottle of cognac, 1 bottle of syrup, 1 small cask of vin ordinaire, 12 lemons, 3 pounds of sugar, 3 pounds of chocolate and 3 pounds of prunes. So much for communal supplies. In addition, each member of the party was provided with 1 pudding, 1 gourd of lemonade, 1 gourd of orangeade, 1 pot of chicken broth. It took several sacks to contain such a quantity of provisions, together with the ropes, tents and utensils needed for camping below the Grands Mulets. There is a certain charm, too, in the elaborate costume which Mademoiselle d'Angeville ordered especially for the ascent. She herself described it as follows: 'It comprised a shirt and knickers of red flannel, one pair of silk and one pair of woollen stockings worn one over the other, strong hobnailed shoes, baggy ankle-length trousers of chequered Scottish wool lined with flannel, a long knee-length smock of the same material gathered with a belt, a fur-trimmed cap and straw hat lined with green cloth, a velvet mask, snow-glasses, a plaid, a fur boa, a fur cape and an alpenstock.' The climb was successful if not over-dramatic, and the correspondent of the *Journal des Débats* reported to his readers from Chamonix: 'Her return was hailed with almost indescribable enthusiasm. Cannon were discharged, the inhabitants of the entire valley flocked to see the heroine, and the name d'Angeville is for ever inscribed beside those of Jacques Balmat and de Saussure.' Henriette had become 'the lioness of elegant and cultivated society... this intrepid tourist... the first and only woman to have undertaken this arduous tour... replies to the questions that come to her from all sides with great charm and much wit.'

Mademoiselle d'Angeville, who made a total of twenty-one ascents, climbed the Oldenhorn when she was sixty-nine. She died at seventy-eight and was buried in Lausanne, 'within sight of the mountains she loved so much'. Not all the nineteenth-century climbers of Mont Blanc seem to have been gripped by her enthusiasm. Paul Verne, whose literary style tempts one to infer a kinship, spiritual if not by blood, with his famous namesake Jules, expatiated in a rather long-winded fashion on the hardships and perils occasioned by his 'fortieth French ascent of Mont Blanc'. He also discovered that, by 1871, guides and porters could not be arbitrarily selected because the all-powerful Chamonix Guild of Guides had an important say in the matter. Having at last completed his highly dramatic tour with the aid of Gaspard Simon and the brothers Edouard and Ambroise Ravanel, he hastened to put mountaineering in a proper light by quoting the blunt comments of a Mr Markham Shervill: 'Be that as it may, I advise no one to make the ascent of Mont Blanc, which, even if successful, bears no reasonable relationship to the dangers which one experiences there and expects of others.' Paul Verne agreed, but was sporting enough to add that, while holding the same view, he hoped it would not be shared. Edouard Ravanel must, incidentally, have been adept in painting a dire picture of the perils and incertitudes of a Mont Blanc ascent because he informed Verne that, only a year before, an entire party – seven guides, three porters and two Englishmen – had reached the summit but perished miserably in a storm. Mark Twain's version of the incident differs in that he speaks of a 'caravan' of eleven persons comprising three guides, five porters, two Americans and a Scotsman. Where numbers, general situation and sequence of events are concerned, one is inclined to place more credence in Twain, a professional journalist, than in Monsieur Paul Verne. The fact remains that it was a serious climbing accident, one which proved that Mont Blanc could be treacherous and, like other peaks, claim lives from time to time. Twain's *A Tramp Abroad,* perhaps the most colourful travel book ever written by a man blessed with a sense of humour, contains an account which illustrates the Mont Blanc story with a narrative freshness that offsets the author's sarcasm. He mentions an ice-cavern nearly a hundred yards long, evidently a principal attraction of the fashionable Mont Blanc tour of his day, and describes how the proprietor suddenly vanished into a side tunnel with his candles 'and left us buried in the bowels of the glacier, and in pitch-darkness. We judged his purpose was murder and robbery; so we got out our matches and prepared to sell our lives as dearly as possible by setting the glacier on fire if the worst came to the worst – but we soon perceived that this man had changed his mind; he began to sing, in a deep, melodious voice, and woke some curious and pleasing echoes.' But not even a sceptic like Mark Twain could escape the beauty and sublimity of the mountains. When it came to describing his alpine experiences, he used truly dithyrambic language: 'Indeed, those mighty bars of alternate light and shadow streaming up from behind that dark and prodigious form and occupying the half of the dull and opaque heavens, was the most impressive and imposing marvel I had ever looked upon. There is no simile for it, for nothing is like it. If a child had asked me what it was, I should have said, "Humble yourself, in this presence, it is the glory flowing from the hidden head of the Creator."'

This may be the proper place to recall a description of a first ascent to glacier snow which, better than almost any other, puts into words the profound and silent potency of the impression left by such an experience. It is the passage in Adalbert Stifter's *Nachsommer* which tells how young Drendorf and his faithful companion Kaspar witness the coming of day in the High Alps. 'As we stood there talking, the mist started to pale at one point in the east, the snowfields became tinged with a lovelier and more agreeable hue than the leaden grey with which they had hitherto been mantled, and in the pale patch of mist there began to glow a dot which grew ever larger until, attaining the size of a plate, it hovered there, dull red but glowing deeply like the fieriest of rubies. It was the sun, which had risen above the lower peaks and was burning through the mist. The snow grew ever redder, ever more distinct, its shadows almost greenish. The tall crags to our right, situated in the west, also sensed the approaching radiance and blushed pink. There was nothing else to be seen save the huge dark sky above us and, standing in the plain expanse that had been set there by Nature, two human beings. ... At last, the mist began to glow like molten metal at its furthest extremity... the sun emerged from its wrappings with the gleam of bronze... the joyful day had come.'

The Bond Between Guide and Climber

The image of alpine climbing, which evolved during the nineteenth century from mere mountain hikes and sporadic high-altitude sorties, is inseparable from the figure of the guide. He became not only the necessary escort and attendant of those who climbed the High Alps in ever-increasing numbers but also the companion and, often enough, fellow-victim of men fascinated by the virgin peaks they sought to conquer. Again and again, the almost mystic bond that unites a roped party helped to overcome obstacles and difficulties which would probably have defeated a solo climber. The 'Matterhorn tragedy', a sequel to the first ascent of that mountain on 14 July 1865 by Edward Whymper and six companions, derives its human pathos from the fact that the four who fell to their deaths during the descent may have been victims of a 'technical failure' (i.e. a weak rope). The incident caused a worldwide stir and provoked talk of human inadequacy, irresponsibility and presumption, of guilt and divine retribution. When all is said and done, the blame may simply have lain with man's urge to tread the untrodden and attain the dazzling objective. As George Leigh Mallory, the hero of Mount Everest, said in answer to the question 'Why?': 'Because it's there.'

This 'it' was stronger than reason, and seeming unreason brought a princely reward: the fulfilment of a dream which liberated man from the lowlands and took him to high places at whose feet lay a whole world of valleys, lakes, villages, forests and people. To a blue and weightless infinity flooded with light.

Once the hazards of mountaineering were recognized, ways and means of overcoming them were devised. Remote valleys, small villages and large tourist centres bred whole generations of guides who leagued themselves with the bold assailants of the Alps. It is impossible to enumerate every great guide and climber who set himself an exceptional target and attained it or found a white death among the mountains, but here are some. Melchior Anderegg, who conquered the Jungfrau; Balmat and Paccard, joint vanquishers of Mont Blanc; Walter Bonatti, the great solo climber; Michel Croz and Jean-Antoine Carrel, both victims of the Matterhorn; the brothers Guglierma and their Monte Rosa; Heinrich Harrer, who first climbed the North Face of the Eiger on 24 June 1938 with F. Kasparek, A. Heckmair and L. Vörg; John Harlin of San Francisco, who followed their example and died; Toni Hiebeler, who conquered the dread face in winter; Misumara Takada, hero of the first Japanese ascent in 1965; five more Japanese, among them a girl, who brought off the spectacular *direttissima* between 15 July and

15 August 1969; Louis Lachanel and Lionel Terray, the expert pair who also won laurels in the Himalayas and Andes; Dr Eugen Guido Lammer, great solo climber of the Eastern Alps; the Frenchman Georges Livanos of Dolomites fame, who achieved 20 years of climbing, 300 first ascents, 18 000 pitons and 38 bivouacs; Carlo Mauri, who distinguished himself in the Dolomites, the Valais and Patagonia as well as on Gasherbrum IV in the Himalayas; Albert Frederick Mummery, rock-climbing virtuoso of the Mont Blanc massif; Tita Piaz, who climbed in the Dolomites; Ludwig Purtscheller, who scaled 1700 peaks in the Western and Eastern Alps and made the first ascent of Kibo, 5930-metre-high main peak of Kilimanjaro; Buhl and Burgener, Cassin and Darbellay, Gaspard and Hemming, Leigh Mallory and Rébuffat, Emile and Guido Rey and Claude Kozan, 'the world's highest woman', who climbed 7700 metres up the flank of Cho Oyu. The list should include many more whose names are now forgotten.

Alpine climbing has had its share of records but they are not beaten as on the race-track or in the stadium, where competitors vie for cheap glory in the presence of sensation-seeking crowds. In 1962, when Darbellay and Vouilloz scaled the north flank of the Matterhorn in six hours fifteen minutes, their feat won most applause from climbers who could judge what it

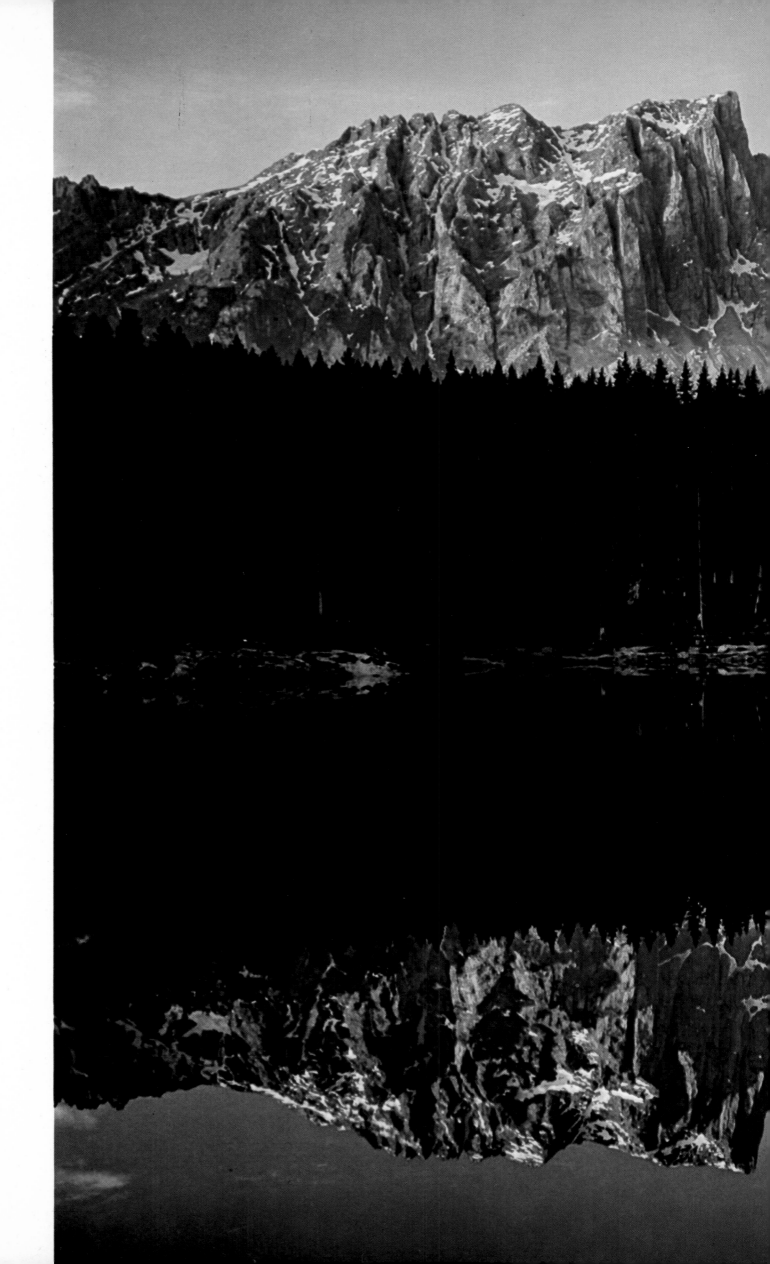

meant in terms of precise and careful work. It earned them respect and recognition, and anyone who knew the mountain rejoiced that their venture had succeeded. Climbers have never really needed eye-witnesses; their word is enough. The steady growth of mountaineering literature during the nineteenth century did not stem from a need to submit written testimony. The pieces in question were personal accounts and descriptions written to the greater glory of the mountains. Many who resorted to print were criers in the urban wilderness. Rousseau's 'back to Nature' influenced this desire to go to the mountains and on upwards to the untouched peaks. What was at first confined mainly to the journals and year-books of mountaineering clubs developed into a mountaineering literature proper. The climber became the hero of a new literary genre, and the guide, calm and taciturn, tough and reliable, emerged as a father figure to whom one entrusted oneself spiritually as well as physically. There came into being a new form of regional novel which, in company with artistically designed mountain roads, beflagged steamers and rack-railways, assured the Alps of ample publicity. The tourist industry invaded even the remotest mountain villages, and wherever a small plot of level ground gave scope for a boarding-house and terrace with a guaranteed view of the alpine sunset, 'Alpenblick' pensions were built. But away from the main tourist routes, health resorts and fashionable mountain hotels, there remained untouched alpine scenery, unexplored and unconquered terrain, and unsolved mountaineering assignments, or 'problems', as they used to be called in the 1880s and 1890s. One of these 'early alpine problems', the north-west face of the Gross-Venediger, was not only solved by that articulate climber Dr Lammer but embodied by him in one of the best-written and, because of its psychological profundity, tensest descriptive pieces in alpine literature. An expedition led by Archduke John of Austria and the guide Rohregger, both of them distinguished contemporary alpinists, had vainly attempted to scale the mountain on 8 August 1828. Lammer approached it with the eyes of a sentimental primitive: 'bleak and grey, tired and heavy, charged with an immense burden of snow, the mists writhed around, and the wind fell silent for minutes on end as though listening.' A little later, already advancing on the unconquered foe: 'By the time I reached the debris-strewn extremity of the north crest, a faintly hopeful pink, soon to be followed by an expectant red, was wreathing the spacious morning-scented atmosphere.' Then the final phase of his solitary climb: 'Ah, that cornice! If I live to be ninety, the ice-cold memory of that hour will still haunt my nightly slumbers.

I cannot dissemble, and will not lie to make myself a hero when in fact I was shaken by the cowardly fear of death. Let others feel no fear as they traverse the cornice in deep powder snow, unroped and unaccompanied save by the ever-present recollection of their own fall from two hundred metres: *homo sum!*'

Only someone who has felt the mist clawing damply at his shoulders or searched the rock-face for a handhold against the sinister possibility of a fall will understand the sentiments of this man, for all their literary garnish, and not be surprised to read what he wrote when he returned unscathed: 'You are a glutton for atmosphere, an artful hedonist; you like to quaff each sensation pure and unalloyed, and, because even the most tactful companion must necessarily distract your senses, you prefer to tread deserted paths in solitude...'

That was in 1891, a year which saw Bismarck's dismissal from public office, the establishment of the 'International Peace Bureau' in Switzerland and the founding of the 'Pan-German Association', a pioneer of the Imperialist movement. Also in the same year, the Prussian general Helmuth von Moltke died, Engels wrote *Die Entwicklung des Sozialismus von der Utopie zur Wissenschaft,* Samuel P. Langley published *Experiments in Aerodynamics* and Lilienthal attempted his first glider flights. Seven years later, Captain Spelterini's balloon soared and swooped from Sitten in the Valais to Rivière in France. Perspectives shift, distances shrink, mountains are reduced to problems of transportation, alpine passes acquire renewed strategic importance and the Alps become an object of warlike speculation. Only the white giants and dark rocks keep silent, their timeless forms enveloped in mist and icy showers.

The Stone Rose-garden

Repeatedly the light breaks through, the mists disperse, the day surges into the dark valleys and the sun brings the meadows, trees and flowers to life. It makes an unforgettable picture. Alpine climbers, few of whom were skilled with words, soon tried to preserve at least a photographic record of their experiences. It was not long before unwieldy plate cameras complete with tripods and black cloths joined the equipment of mountaineers whose fathers had carried crayon and sketchbook. Although many of their pictures were intended to illustrate tour reports, serve as pictorial guides or contribute to alpine exploration, they were inevitably tempted to capture the beauty of the mountains, the fleeting moment, in the form of pictorial souvenirs. For a long time, black-and-white photography not only did justice to the subject but produced expert photographers whose pictures helped transmit their experiences to those who could not scale the highest peaks. The Japanese photographer Yoshikazu Shirakawa has chosen to convey such experiences in colour-pictures of exceptional power and impact: the blue-green chill of frozen wastes, the sky awakening to light and colour at daybreak, dizzy depths, peaks glowing at sunrise, rocks on fire with the sun's last rays. Shirakawa is not content to reproduce the peaceful mountainside: what he imparts is the vision of a world in flames.

Years ago in Merano I met a girl who told me of a strange spectacle she had witnessed 'somewhere above Bolzano'. Standing outside her hotel at dusk, she saw the mountains opposite 'start to burn', but not with the incandescent red of a furnace. It was as though a rosy haze had issued from the rock and settled over everything like a warm, peaceful radiance. The girl's account bore witness to an experience which many have shared: the sight of limestone ridges, rocky towers and pinnacles glowing pink in the sun's last rays like rose-gardens of stone bedded in dark porphyry.

The Dolomites are different, as every climber will confirm. For some, the experienced, tireless and iron-nerved, a climber's paradise. For those who seek peace and seclusion, a world which affords a view of a different and more southern landscape. Others, again, may have been captivated by their names, which transcend the language barrier: La Marmolata, Monte Cristallo, Tofane, Croda Rossa, Sasso Lungo, Punta Tasca.

One man of my acquaintance, who has to spend eleven months out of twelve in the smog and turmoil of a big city, put it this way: 'Your Alps are Nature's richest horn of plenty.' Being an American, he hopes to see a sizable conservation area established complete with mountain guides, guaranteed sunsets, high-altitude ski slopes, wrestling contests, alpine festivals, mineral springs, cow-bells, the scent of pine-resin and, down in the valleys, Hilton hotels in chalet style. The worthy man, most of whose requirements are already met, forgot one thing, that there still exist people who expect the Alps to give them something not to be found in any guide-book: an encounter with natural beauty, unspoiled by roads, mountain railways and ski-lifts. These are the quiet people who still find time for an evening chat with the peasant outside his hut; people to whom an alpine meadow full of flowers, and butterflies, conveys more than the celebrated Grand Tour of the Four Passes; people who take greater pleasure in a fragment of rock-crystal than in any diamond necklace. They are privileged to make discoveries which leave them richer and happier, like the man who returned again and again to the rock-drawings in the Val Camonica, cult-symbols which pre-historic man had scratched on the rock thousands of years before, strange shapes, hunters' conjurations, pictorial appeals to gods and spirits. What did he care if their significance escaped him? It was enough for him to feel that the mountains had once been inhabited by people for whom they may have provided a last refuge, hunters who roused huge cave-bears with flaming brands and dispatched them with stone axes and wooden spears. Historians and scholars have told of megaliths and paving-stones, of huts built on piles beside alpine lakes, of hot springs that have bubbled from the ground for thousands of years, exhaled from the depths of the earth's crust, which sometimes stirs like a slumbering giant and causes the ground to quake.

The primeval landscape of the Alps is inexhaustible. The Swiss may have named a thousand glaciers, calculated the height of every peak, impounded alpine streams in reservoirs, built roads through passes or pierced mountains with railway tunnels. Yet beyond the furthest herdsman's hut in the remotest alpine valley rise the mountains which tolerate or reject human presence, mysterious, moody and treacherous, ever-changing and ever unspoiled. To know them, one must experience their menace and enchantment, see the wind draw a veil of falling water across dark rocks, feel the valley tremble to the thunder of an avalanche, climb, too, to heights where everything human is left behind and, in utter silence, white peaks support a crystalline sky that is the roof of an entire continent.

122

Plates on pages 13-40

In the case of mountain groups, the altitude given is always that of the highest peak. The numerals on the maps are page numbers.

13   Photograph taken from the cable railway linking Chamonix (1037 m) with the Aiguilles du Midi (3843 m): view of the Aiguille Verte (4127 m).

14/15   Mont Blanc massif (aerial photograph). Left to right: Aiguille du Géant (4013 m), the main peak of Mont Blanc (4807 m), Mont Maudit and Mont Blanc du Tacul (4248 m). In the foreground, the Glacier de Leschaux on Mont Mallet.

16/17   Ice-fall of the Glacier du Géant: background right, the Tour Ronde (3792 m).

18/19   The Glacier d'Argentière. Background left, Mont Dolant (3821 m); centre, the Aiguille du Triolet (3870 m).

20/21   View from Lac Blanc, west of Chamonix, of the Grandes Jorasses (4208 m) and the Aiguille du Géant (4013 m). On the right of the picture, the Aiguilles de Chamonix.

22/23   Looking eastwards across Lac Blanc. Left to right: Aiguille Verte, Aiguille du Dru, Grandes Jorasses, Aiguille du Géant, Aiguilles de Chamonix and the summit of Mont Blanc.

24   A section of the Aiguilles de Chamonix, photographed from the valley.

25   The Refuge Vallot (4362 m) on the way up Mont Blanc.

26/27   Sunset over the Dôme du Goûter (4304 m).

28/29   North face of the Grandes Jorasses (4208 m) with the Aiguille du Géant on the right.

This picture was taken from the Refuge du Couvercle (2687 m).

30/31   Left, the Aiguille du Tour (3540 m) and Glacier du Tour; right, the Aiguille Chardonnet (3824 m). Taken just before sunset.

32/33   Ridge of firn below the summit of Mont Blanc (4807 m).

34/35   The Grandes Jorasses and Dent du Géant; on the right, the Col du Géant and glacier of the same name.

36   View of the Glacier du Bossons from the Aiguilles du Midi.

37   Ridge leading to the summit of Mont Blanc.

38/39   The Aiguilles du Midi photographed from the village of Planpraz.

40   The frozen side of the Aiguille d'Argentière (3896 m).

Plates on pages 49-76

49 View from the Riffelalp, showing the Obergabelhorn (4063 m), Wellenkuppe and Zinalrothorn (4221 m) in the Valais.

50/51 Traditional view of the mighty pyramid of the Matterhorn (4477 m), here reflected in the Riffelsee.

52/53 Panoramic view across the Gorner Glacier. Left to right: Nordend, Dufourspitze (4634 m), Grenzgletscher, Lyskamm, Castor and Pollux.

54/55 This is how Monte Rosa's Dufourspitze looks when the sun has already set and the topmost peaks glow red in the dying light.

56/57 Looking across the Gorner Glacier (here seen from Monte Rosa): Matterhorn, Dent Blanche (4357 m) and Obergabelhorn.

58/59 Flying over the mountains of the Valais.

60/61 The huge icy serpent of the Aletsch Glacier (27 km long), with the Grosses Aletschhorn (4195 m) on the left of the picture. Top right, the Jungfrau (4158 m), Jungfraujoch and Mönch. Taken from the Eggishorn, facing north.

62 Grindelwald, overlooked by the massive Wetterhorn (3701 m).

63 The North Face of the Eiger: a foreshortened view from the Kleine Scheidegg.

64/65 Eiger (3970 m) and Mönch (4099 m). At the lower edge of the picture, the Kleine Scheidegg.

66 The Grosses Luteraarhorn and Schreckhorn (4078 m).

67 The sun blazing up over the Mönch.

68/69 A new day dawns over the Wetterhorn.

70/71 The Bachalpsee, and above it the Gross Schreckhorn and Finsteraarhorn (4274 m).

72/73 The huge pyramid of the Weisshorn (4506 m) in the Valais.

74/75 Health resort of the rich and famous: St Moritz (1823 m) showing the Muotas Muragl, Piz Muragl (3157 m), Piz Languard (3262 m) and Piz Albris (3166 m).

76 Memorable view from the Sphinx-Terrasse of the Jungfraujoch and the Bernese Alps in the west.

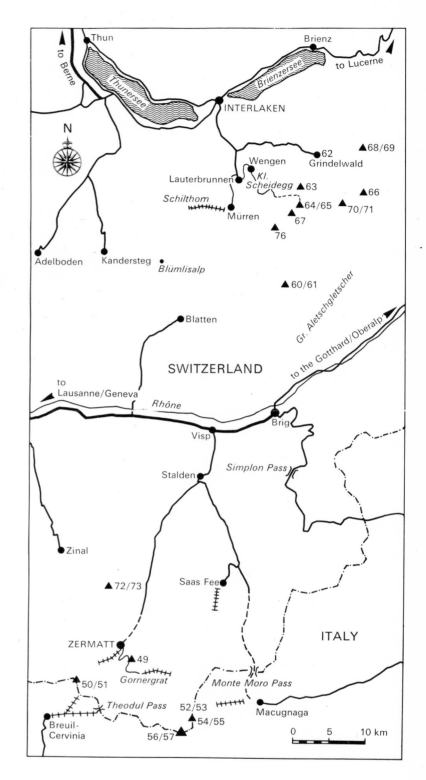

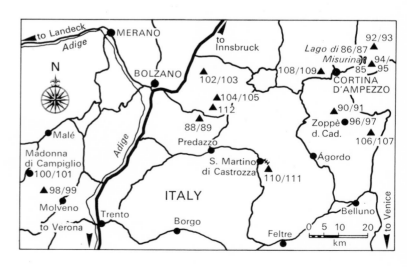

134

Plates on pages 85-112

Plates on pages 121-132

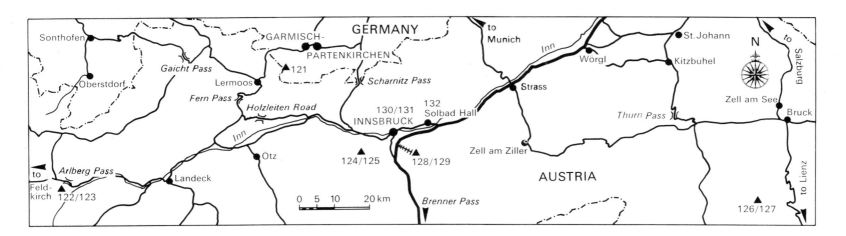

Yoshikazu Shirakawa

Born in 1935 at Kawanoe, Japan, Shirakawa completed his studies in the photographic department of the Nihon University College of Art in 1957. The same year he became an assistant in the 'Literature and Art' section of the Nippon Broadcasting System Inc. and in 1958 chief camera-man of the Fuji Telecasting Company, Ltd. He has been working as a free-lance photographer since 1960.

As head of a section dealing with special photographic assignments, he visited a total of 130 countries to collect material for *Culture and Geography of the World* (23 volumes) and *World Culture Series* (26 volumes). His photographic achievements have won him several awards from associations and official bodies, among them the 1972 Mainichi Art Prize (for his photographs of the Himalayas) and the Art Prize of the Ministry of Education.

Shirakawa's work has been exhibited no less than twelve times in his native Japan. He is a member of the Japan Photography Association and the Japan Mountain Club and a lecturer at the Nihon Photography School.

Cameras used: ASAHI PENTAX 6×7

Lenses used: Super Takumar F. 3.5/55 mm,
F. 4.5/75 mm, F. 2.4/105 mm,
F. 4/200 mm.

136